PROTECT YOUR MIND

A Middle-Aged Adult Guide to
Dementia Prevention

DR. EVON ANUKAM

DISCLAIMER

While this book provides research-based information on how to prevent or reduce the risk of getting Alzheimer's dementia, it does not guarantee the intended result. The book is for informational purposes and does not constitute or replace health or medical advice from your health care provider.

ACKNOWLEDGMENTS

I owe a debt of gratitude to my husband, children, and one of my best friends, Amaka Orji, who cheered me on as I wrote this book. I'm extremely grateful to my sister, Rev Sr Gertrude, for exposing me to life in the convent and for showing me how she and most nuns live and age with full brain function. I would also like to thank my friend and co-worker Dr Patricia Fogarty who directed me to some of the best resources to get my research information for this book. I extend my appreciation to my longtime friend and colleague, Dr Evelyne Chiakpo, who offered her initial opinion on the manuscript and went on to write the foreword for this book. I also wish to express my sincere thanks to my friends, who became family, Sam Okafor, Nwanneka Mbelu, and my sister friend, Eucharia Iheme, who visited, offered undying support, and encouraged me while I cared for my mother in my home. Finally, I give special thanks to my coach, Dr Shola Ezeokoli, whose guidance, direction, and expertise paved the way for this book to be completed.

FOREWORD

Dementia is a well-known chronic scourge that takes away cognitive functions in older folks and significantly affects their quality of life. There are various etiologies, some identifiable, some not but the most common is Alzheimer's. It is well known that this disease unfortunately also impacts family members and care givers.

This book is a beautifully written guide from a health literate lens and as such gives us a unique perspective.

The advice given not only gives a better understanding of the struggle of our loved ones but also helps manage the care giver's stress and facilitates communication between the various multi-disciplinary members of the team usually involved. It, therefore, makes us better advocate for our loved ones and ourselves.

Additionally, it details various non-pharmacological remedies and lifestyle changes to improve our wellbeing whether we are at risk for dementia or not. That is a plus, especially because it comes from a medical expert who not only is an active and dutiful care giver but researched ways to improve her wellbeing and minimize her potential future risks.

This book provides tips for self-care and stress management that are inevitable when one is an active care giver. There are lots of unknown and unpredictable behaviors and watching memories fading, personality changing, and quality of life deteriorating are not easy to deal with. It empowers the care giver to be able to recognize that and be patient with our affected loved ones.

Lifestyle modifications recommended include regular exercises, improved social interaction, healthy food fairs, sleep hygiene and cognitive stimulation. The author walks us through her own journey with tips on how to sustain these new choices. The author makes it clear to seek advice from your PCP before embarking on these changes. It is also a succinct way to have an enriched encounter at an annual physical encounter or visits to address well-known chronic ailments like diabetes, hypertension, hyperlipidemia, and weight management.

Overall, it is well written and rich with a unique view from an active care giver who shared her personal experiences.

Evelyne Chiakpo, MD
Family Medicine Physician and Clinical Associate Professor

ENDORSEMENTS

As a palliative care doctor, I care for patients with dementia. I witness the arduous journey their families endure. Dr Anukam's succinct description will help inspire the middle-aged, now including Millennials, to adopt a 'dementia prevention lifestyle', so they might avoid this life changing disease.

Patricia Fogarty, MD
Palliative Physician, Providence Health and Services

A beautifully written expose of a health literate care giver's experience learning and supporting a family member through the journey. A succinct and unique perspective on healthy lifestyle changes to mitigate the devastating effects of this chronic ailment

Evelyne Chiakpo, MD
Family Medicine Physician and Clinical Associate Professor

An essential educational tool in the battle against Alzheimer's disease, this book brings light to a difficult subject: Am I doomed to get Alzheimer's? Written with families of Alzheimer's patients

*in mind, Dr Anukam draws from personal experience and clini-
cal research to develop an easy to read and understand book with
practical suggestions on how to reduce your risk of developing
Alzheimer's disease.*

Suzanne Anthony, RPh, retired hospital pharmacist

*Dr Evon Anukam has written an insightful and timely book
that can guide people who provide care for their loved ones with
dementia and those who seek to protect themselves from experiencing this devastating illness. It is written with the validity
of an experienced clinical pharmacist and the vulnerability of a
lived experience. This book is highly recommended.*

**Ucheoma Nwizu, PharmD, BCACP, MEd.
Clinical Pharmacy Manager**

*In a very succinct way, Dr Evon Anukam, through a lived ex-
perience of her mother's dementia journey, makes clear the need
to prevent this monster disease*

Nwanneka Mbelu, Retired Registered Nurse

DEDICATION

This book is dedicated to my mother, Regina. She lost her husband, my dad, in her prime but she showed strength, courage, and resilience as she charted a new path toward life. She played a major role in my children's lives both when I was in graduate school and while I built my career. She continued to be a constant presence in our lives. Her diagnosis with Alzheimer's dementia was very difficult but we came together as a family and made sure that she would continue to feel our love as she journeys through this new unpredictable territory.

CONTENTS

INTRODUCTION

I have been a healthcare professional for over two decades, and as such have come across many diseases that people have and live with on a regular basis. One of those diseases is dementia. With most diseases such as diabetes, high blood pressure, high cholesterol, mental health etc., healthcare providers educate patients on preventive measures to lower their risks for such diseases. However, dementia is not one of them. Conversations about dementia begin when a family member is diagnosed, and they usually revolve around the issues and challenges surrounding care of the patient suffering from dementia. I was guilty of this norm. That is, until I noticed that my highly independent, sophisticated mother was beginning to show signs of cognitive decline and was ultimately diagnosed with Alzheimer's dementia or Alzheimer's disease. After getting over the initial shock of my mother's diagnosis and positioning her to receive the ongoing care she would need, I made it a personal mission to go back in time to not only look at what the research showed, but to also do what I needed to do, and by whatever means necessary to lower my risk of dementia. The more I gain all the useful knowledge about how to keep my brain healthy and active, the more optimistic I am about living a dementia-free life. I thought about people like me, all the middle-aged men and women, between the ages of 40-65, with a new family history of dementia, suddenly are faced with the responsibility of taking care of elderly parents with dementia. I also thought about those who do not have family histories and mistakenly think that they do not have to be concerned about getting dementia. I decided that this book will serve the purpose of creating awareness and providing the right tools on how to prevent dementia. It is a book with practical information and ideas to help people navigate through life and look forward to aging without the fear of getting dementia.

1

The Silent Threat:
Understanding
Alzheimer's Disease

My mom is a vibrant larger than life woman. Over a period of a year to a year and half, I started to notice some memory lapses when we spoke on the phone. She would forget some parts of the conversation we had the day before or she would deny having any conversation at all. At first, I did not make anything of it, although, in retrospect, I realized that I was in denial that my mom could be losing her memory, until she was diagnosed with mild dementia. Nothing was the same again after learning this official diagnosis. Having prior experience dealing with patients with dementia did not make my own family experience any easier but the latter became a wakeup call for me. I suddenly realized that I must take some action, although I did not know what type of action at the time. After going through an adjustment period, I went in full force and educated myself. To approach any disease or problem, the first order of business is to understand the "what, where, when, and how", of that disease. And that is exactly what I did. And what I want to share with you and anyone else who picks up this book to learn more about how to work toward staving off dementia for as long as one possibly can.

What is dementia?

Dementia is a consistent, irreversible, and progressive loss of brain faculties that control our thinking, memory, language, and reasoning. As such, lack of these basic brain functions negatively affects an individual's day-to-day activities and living.

There are four major types of dementia: Alzheimer's, Lewy Body, Vascular, and frontotemporal. Alzheimer's disease is the most common form of dementia, especially in older adults. Due to my family history of Alzheimer's (my mom has it), this book will focus primarily on this type of dementia.

Alzheimer's dementia is a rapidly growing disease and seen as the second most worrisome and feared disease in the US, after cancer. It affects 7 million people in the United States; and 50 million worldwide and is expected to reach 152 million people by the year 2050. It robs one in ways that other diseases do not, by shutting down the basic function of the brain, while creating a heavy financial, physical, and emotional burden on family members and those entrusted with the care of the Alzheimer's patient.

Alzheimer's Disease

Alzheimer's disease can present as early onset, affecting those in the younger age category of 45-60 years, and late onset which affects those 65 and older. Although Alzheimer's affects the younger population (early onset), up to 85% of cases are 75 years and older (late onset).

Alzheimer's disease is the 5th leading cause of death in adults 65 years and older after heart disease, cancer, stroke and chronic lung disease. In the United States, the healthcare costs for Alzheimer's disease were estimated at $321 billion in 2022 and expected to reach $1 trillion by 2050, excluding indirect costs from loss of income, unpaid caregiving, and expenses incurred by family members on behalf of the patient. I had the opportunity to care for my mother while she was in the mild stages of Alzheimer's dementia. Although she still functioned well at this stage, she had an incident that worsened her disease. This required me to take a long leave of absence to care for her. When it was time to go back to work, I looked for a caregiver to come to my home to take care of her Monday through Friday from morning to evening. The cheapest caregiver I could get cost $4000 a month, paid out of pocket, since it was not covered by health insurance. This unbudgeted expense put a lot of financial strain on our family. This, in addition to other indirect home expenses and the fact that I was still her primary caregiver from the time I came home from work and on the weekends. Fortunately, my mom's situation became less severe over time, but it still took close to nine months. Regarding the emotional burden, a friend once told me that her Alzheimer's mom had recurring erratic behavior that she just wanted to give up on her mother and herself and end it all. But she stayed strong enough to call for help when her mom became violent toward her.

As we age, our brain cells naturally start to decline. This is a normal process that happens for various reasons including: low/no estrogen, as seen in menopause, and low testosterone production. Afterall, nothing lives forever. In Alzheimer's disease, a protein called beta-amyloid produces plaques (clusters or clumps) in the brain that would cause death of brain cells. A second protein called tau becomes altered and disrupts neurons (the information messengers to and from the brain). Following accumulation of these toxic proteins, it takes about ten to twenty years to start to see signs of mild dementia. At this later stage, hippocampus, the part of the brain that controls memory, learning, and emotion, becomes damaged by these toxic proteins and as such its function also starts to decline.

Some genetic markers called APOE have been identified as the category of genes that make a person vulnerable to Alzheimer's disease, with APOE type 4 being the most recognized risk marker, based on the number of copies of the APOE4 gene that a person carries. The more copies an individual has, the higher the risk. People can get tested for these genes if they choose to do so. Knowing that I have a family history of Alzheimer's disease, I thought about getting tested for these genes but later opted not to. Since I was determined to take preventive measures toward Alzheimer's, I felt that knowing my results would not change any plans I put in place for myself.

Alzheimer's disease, like any other disease, comes with certain risk factors. These are discussed in detail in chapter 3 of this book.

There is currently no cure for dementia. In a typical Alzheimer's patient, life expectancy from initial presentation of symptoms to death is 8-10 years. No one wants to live the last ten years of their lives losing their mind but this, unfortunately, is what happens with those with Alzheimer's disease.

Alzheimer's dementia falls into three categories: mild, moderate, and severe.

In the mild stage, the individual finds it difficult to remember common vocabulary. Familiar objects suddenly become unfamiliar. Confusion and misplacement of objects become quite noticeable. There are some mood swings and less interest in common activities. The mild stage varies from individual to individual, but most people are still functional at this early stage.

During the moderate stage, the individual is more forgetful and more confused and needs assistance with most aspects of care.

In the severe stage, there's a total loss of independence and ability to communicate. It involves both physical decline, which would require total care, and total loss of brain function.

Alzheimer's affects quality and pattern of sleep. At the early stages of her disease my mom fractured her hip due to a fall. The trauma pushed her Alzheimer's temporarily to a moderate phase. She would wake up every hour confused and frustrated because she did not know where she was. Her waking up also meant that her caregiver, who was me at the time, would have to wake up to tend to her needs.

Patients undergo major personality changes; they have difficulty speaking and processing their thoughts; they cannot follow simple commands; they become aggressive toward loved ones. Some end up dying undignified deaths. Family members deal with the emotional roller coaster of watching their loved ones become someone they no longer recognize.

This is hopefully when you finally say to yourself, if you have not already, that you will do everything in your power to ensure you do not get Alzheimer's. No one wants to put their family through the agony of watching someone they love to go through this disease. I made this decision at the early stages of my mom's Alzheimer's case. You need not wait for your loved one or yourself to get this diagnosis before you act.

2

Dispelling Myths:
What Alzheimer's Dementia Is Not

How many times have you forgotten a name or situation and thought you had dementia? We leave our car keys or cellphones, or even park our cars in places we do not recall, and we sometimes swear we are experiencing dementia. You walk into a room to get something, and you instantly forget why you were there in the first place, and then, you panic and think you are surely losing your mind. The fear that we associate with dementia or cognitive impairment may lead us to attribute some of these temporary memory lapses and momentary forgetfulness to dementia. In the examples cited above, the assumption of dementia is both unrealistic and invalid. Forgetting where you parked your car or left your car keys or what you came into a room to fetch, are natural occurrences that can happen to anyone. It is a misconception to believe that memory should be systematic and that recall of past events should be straightforward. Sometimes we engage in selective memory for different reasons. I am guilty of accusing my husband of invoking his selective memory when he does not remember an important conversation. If we become more aware of our distractions, these forms of forgetfulness will lessen. There are a few other myths or misconceptions that people have about Alzheimer's dementia:

Myth One: I am developing Alzheimer's dementia because I am becoming more forgetful with age.

Being forgetful is part of the aging process. Alzheimer's disease is different because it involves consistent forgetfulness and making poor judgments and decisions that are sometimes detrimental to one's life. The United States Centers for Disease Control (CDC) published some basic warning signs of Alzheimer's that warrant a visit to the doctor's office:

- Your forgetfulness affects your daily life.
- You experience challenges in problem-solving and planning normal day-to-day activities.
- You have difficulty completing familiar home tasks.
- You cannot locate misplaced items.
- You experience word-finding difficulties.

Myth Two: Alzheimer's drugs can reverse the disease.

There is currently no cure for Alzheimer's disease. However, there are a few prescription drugs including, Donepezil (Aricept), Galantamine (Razadyne), and Namenda (Memantine) that serve the purpose of slowing Alzheimer's disease progression. These class of medications, called cholinesterase inhibitors, do come with some side effects that include weight gain, urinary disturbance, increased or decreased blood pressure, aggressive behavior and some nausea, vomiting, and diarrhea. A newer injectable prescription drug, lecanemab-irmb (Leqembi), given as an infusion may be offered to those in the early stages of Alzheimer's. None of these drugs can reverse Alzheimer's disease.

Myth Three: Vaccines can cause Alzheimer's.

This myth may have originated from a study in Canada that found that risk of dementia rose in people that received influenza or pneumococcal vaccination. But this study has since been debunked because the way the study was designed and conducted created so many biases and inconsistencies. On the contrary, some studies suggest that people who received tetanus and diphtheria vaccine, shingles vaccine, pneumococcal and influenza vaccines were less likely to develop Alzheimer's disease than peers who did not.

Conditions and substances that mimic dementia

In middle-aged and older people, there are conditions or substances that may precipitate symptoms of dementia. Unlike Alzheimer's dementia, these symptoms are reversible when the problem is removed or fixed.

1. Infections: Urinary tract infections and lung infections can worsen brain function, especially in older adults. But when the individual is adequately treated, the infection resolves, along with all cognitive symptoms. It has been suggested that certain infections such as herpes, shingles, Epstein-Barr virus can be linked to Alzheimer's later in life, but this assumption remains controversial and is beyond the scope of this book.

2. Hypothyroidism: A disease in which the body does not produce enough thyroid hormones to meet its metabolic needs, can be mistaken for dementia if undiagnosed and untreated because some of the symptoms mimic dementia. When treated appropriately, thyroid function can be restored, and symptoms reversed.

3. Medications: The effects and side effects from certain medications can mimic dementia, but when recognized and discontinued, affected individuals will usually regain their brain function. The list includes but is

not limited to: Benzodiazepines such as Diazepam (or Valium) and Alprazolam (or Xanax), Antihistamines such as Diphenhydramine (or Benadryl) and Cetirizine (or Zyrtec), Anticholinergics such as Dicyclomine (or Bentyl) and Benztropine (or Cogentin), Tricyclic antidepressants such as Amitriptyline (or Elavil) and Doxepin (Sinequan), Narcotics such Oxycodone (or Oxycontin) and Hydrocodone/Acetaminophen (or Norco), Antidepressants such as Paroxetine (or Paxil) and Fluoxetine (or Prozac) and Anticonvulsants such as Carbamazepine (or Tegretol) and Phenytoin (or Dilantin).

As stated earlier, the list is not exhaustive; people also respond differently to medications. It is important to recognize when a medication is contributing to memory loss, and precipitating signs of dementia.

4. Vitamin levels: Low levels of vitamins B6, B12 and D have been suggested to play a role in reduced brain function. Before people are diagnosed with dementia, their levels of these three vitamins are checked to make sure they are within range. If any or all of them are low, then diagnosis of dementia may not be made. Supplementation of these vitamins is usually warranted to maintain levels within acceptable range. This does not infer that taking these supplements will prevent dementia because studies have

not shown that. But it does indicate that low levels can mimic symptoms that may lead to a false dementia diagnosis. Therefore, it is important to use vitamin supplements if your test results show that they are low.

3

Don't Be Complacent:
Understand Your Risks

I f you ask about ten middle-aged men and women what their risk factors for dementia are, I will bet you that half may not know, and the ones that do may not know the exact number of risk factors.

What are risk factors?

Risk factors are those conditions or behavior or inherited characteristics that make a person more likely to acquire a disease. The more risk factors a person has, the greater the chances of getting the disease. There are some risks we can control and some we cannot control. Most research on prevention is focused on things that we can control. Controllable risk factors contribute up to 50% of most cases of Alzheimer's disease and dementia in general. Our ability to put some action on those areas that we can control may limit the effects of non-controllable risks factors.

Controllable risk factors for Alzheimer's disease are:

Midlife obesity: Obesity is challenging at any age, but it is especially risky in middle age as far as dementia is concerned. Obesity is when your body mass index (BMI) is greater than 30. Fortunately for me, I have never been obese in my lifetime, but I recognize that obesity is prevalent in the United States and is a main contributing factor to heart disease, stroke, diabetes, and some cancers. It is now understood that excess body fat in mid-life can lead to brain shrinkage, which is a common observation in the brains of patients with Alzheimer's dementia.

Hypertension: Hypertension or high blood pressure is a precursor to many diseases that ultimately affect brain function. Once someone is diagnosed with high blood pressure, the condition is considered chronic. However, blood pressure mostly presents a risk for Alzheimer's dementia if it is both chronically high and uncontrolled. The recommended blood pressure for most adults is less than 120/80 mmHg. This number can vary throughout the day based on an individual's routine. However, when blood pressure is consistently higher than 140/90 mmHg, it is diagnosed as high blood pressure or hypertension.

Diabetes: Just like high blood pressure, a diagnosis of diabetes is chronic but mostly creates problems if it is uncontrolled. Normal fasting blood glucose is 70-99mg/dl. Hemoglobin A1C (HbA1c) is another blood test used to screen if a person has prediabetes or diabetes. Normal range for Hemoglobin A1C is 4.8-5.6%. One is considered prediabetic if their Hemoglobin A1C falls between 5.7-6.4% and diabetic if their hemoglobin is equal to or greater than 6.5%.

High cholesterol: High cholesterol can contribute to damage of small blood vessels in the brain, which can contribute to dementia. Normal cholesterol ranges from 100-199mg/dl. Cholesterol level that falls within 200-239mg/dl puts one at a moderate risk while greater than or equal to 240mg/dl puts an individual at high-risk category for heart disease and by default higher risk for dementia.

Smoking: Tobacco smoke in any form is hazardous to health. It is associated with lung cancer, COPD, heart disease; it can also contribute to dementia.

Alcohol Consumption: It is no secret that excess alcohol consumption can be detrimental to health. Along with causing liver failure, pancreatic diseases, and some gastrointestinal disorders, it also promotes dementia. On the other hand, a small glass (2 to 4 ounces) of wine a day may be protective of heart disease and dementia.

Sedentary lifestyle: Physical inactivity is associated with increased risk of Alzheimer's.

Lower level of education: Research shows that people with higher level of education have less Alzheimer's than those with lower level of education. This can be explained by the fact that brain cells can divide to form new cells if they are kept active through active and lifelong learning.

Social isolation: There is not enough evidence to suggest that lack of social interaction and activity leads to the development of dementia. However, social participation improves overall health which in turn may have a positive effect on brain function and vitality.

Chronic stress and depression: Responding to stress is a part of life's normal physiologic states but staying in a chronic state of stress can contribute to dementia. Sometimes stress can lead to depression, and untreated depression can also lead to an increased risk of Alzheimer's dementia. A study published in Alzheimer's Research journal found that cumulative effect of stress is a potential risk for Alzheimer's dementia. This claim is in line with previous studies that also found that stress and depression are contributors to the development of dementia

Nutrition: Maintaining a healthy balanced diet is a lifestyle suitable for reducing the risk of dementia. Eating excess saturated fat and sugar and other foods in the category of junk food can increase the risk of dementia. Some unsaturated fat found in nuts, seeds, avocados and oily fish found in salmon and sardines, otherwise known as omega-3 fatty acids, are good fats and important in your diet.

Non-controllable risk factors for Alzheimer's disease are:

Age: Because the risks increase as we get older, age is the strongest risk factor for Alzheimer's dementia.

Family history: If you have/had parents with Alzheimer's, it means the gene could be passed on to you. This risk is nonexistent when a parent is diagnosed with Alzheimer's after age 80. On the other hand, people that lost their parents from other causes before said parents turned 65 years cannot rule out parental history because they cannot rule out the existence of disease in their family lineage.

The gene passed on from parents is most likely APOE4. Although this gene places one at a higher risk for Alzheimer's than someone without the gene marker, it does not mean that anyone with the gene will get Alzheimer's dementia. I read about someone in the UK who expressed the fact that they had a copy of the APOE4 gene and couldn't help but feel doomed. She went on to state that at least living in Europe allows her to get euthanized if she must and that would be a better way for her to go than to live mindlessly. I also know a friend of a friend who took their life at the young age of 18 because both his mother and grandmother had Alzheimer's dementia. These actions and thinking show how scared and concerned people are about getting the disease. But one can also look at this from a different perspective, one of which is the fact that there are preventive measures that can be taken that would offer one the confidence to believe that their risk of dementia will be less even when they harbor APOE4 gene. There have been reports of those with APOE4 gene that did not get Alzheimer's. Many of them also took protective measures.

Female gender: Females are two times more likely than men to get Alzheimer's. Because women live longer than men, and since the prevalence of Alzheimer's disease increases with age, this trend is expected to keep rising through the years.

People of color: Within the United States, Hispanic Americans have highest risk than other ethnic groups. Black Americans have higher risk than Caucasians but lesser risk than Hispanic Americans while native Americans have higher risks than Caucasians but lesser risks than other groups.

While researchers are actively looking for a cure of Alzheimer's, for now, the best possible solution is to lower our risks, and possibly prevent disease symptoms for as long as possible.

Knowing exactly what your risk factors are will guide you to take the necessary steps to mitigate them.

4

Science to the Rescue: Breakthroughs in Dementia Prevention

There is growing evidence, especially in recent times, to show that we can prevent, delay, or lower our risk of developing dementia. Most of the evidence relates to making changes in bad health behavior, and the use of programs that target the mind. An old saying goes. "prevention is better than cure", and a newer saying goes: "preventing a problem is healthcare". While we await a cure for dementia, it behooves on us to be proactive, by utilizing available research that has shown positive outcome to brain health. I discuss measures from many of these studies below.

PHYSICAL EXERCISE

Numerous studies have shown the benefit of physical aerobic exercise to the aging brain. One study done in several centers in the United States and Australia compared the temporal lobe (part of the brain that controls memory, emotion, and language) of non-demented middle-aged and older adults who consistently engaged in physical activity with the lobes of those who did not exercise. By measuring the thickness of the temporal lobe before and after the study, investigators showed that physically inactive adults had less thickness in their temporal lobes compared to those who were physically active. The thickness of the brain's temporal lobes is suggestive of improved and/or preserved brain function

DANCING

Using dancing as a form of physical exercise, researchers enrolled 60-79 years old inactive men in dancing lessons. They studied the changes in their brains over a six-month period using brain scans and made comparisons to those who were not active dancers. Those in the dancing group showed improvement in the parts of the brain responsible for memory recall and problem-solving, as well as further boost in physical function.

FINGER TRIAL

A large study in Finland called FINGER trial used a combination of diet, exercise, and mind training in elderly subjects to show that those who were randomly assigned to these interventions showed improvements in brain functional scales. This study is now being replicated worldwide and gaining major international recognition.

ACTIVE TRIAL

A short-term, 10-week study with older adults showed that improved performance on activities of daily living was prominent among those who received training in reasoning. This study called The ACTIVE trial had almost 3000 people participate, and the outcome was sustained for at least five years.

LIFESTYLE

A United Kingdom study that tracked older adults for almost ten years looked at genetic risk for Alzheimer's and lifestyle status that included physical activity, healthy food consumption, limited alcohol intake and no smoking. The study found that a healthy way of living reduced the risk of getting Alzheimer's disease, even among those with moderate risk from the Alzheimer's gene.

MODERATE PHYSICAL ACTIVITY

An article published in the Journal of Epidemiology and Community health described the result of a survey where a link was established between doing moderate to vigorous physical activity (MVPA) for 6-10 minutes daily and improvement in memory and cognitive skills. Cognitive skills observed are planning, prioritizing, and organizing. These skills tend to be lacking in Alzheimer's patients. Some of the moderate exercises used are fast walking, stair climbing, slow jogging; and vigorous exercises are fast jogging, swimming, cycling, etc. This research and others like it show that these types of exercises can increase hippocampus in the brain (which plays a major role in learning and memory) even in later years which ultimately can prevent or slow memory loss.

THE NUN STUDY

My sister is a Nun, as in Catholic Reverend sister, so I was excited to read about a study called the Nun study. The Nun study followed a group of 678 elderly nuns of the School Sisters of Notre Dame congregation by looking back in time about early and middle life risk factors for Alzheimer's and following them till death. Nuns live in a convent as a community, dedicating their lives to religious service. They come from different parts of the world and come together to live under one roof. I have had the privilege to visit and spend time with my sister and 15–20 something other nuns that she lives with. I am perplexed by the way they all pray together several times a day, and live and work in peace and harmony. Granted most people cannot live the life of nuns, there is much to be said about the impact of their way of living on their brain function. One of the aspect of nuns' lives that this Nun study looked at was whether speaking multiple languages can lower the risk of dementia. Because the nuns come from different cultural and language origin, they adapt to learning new languages probably more frequently than regular people. They communicate to each other in the language of their host country while also using their native languages or other languages when warranted. One of the observations made and the conclusion reached was that nuns who spoke multiple languages were less likely to develop dementia than those who spoke only one language. The reason this makes sense is that switching from one language to the other requires some brain adjustment that is not notable when only one language is spoken.

FOOD

Food is no stranger to research. Many people have written about the importance of what we consume to our overall health. How and what we eat can increase our risk for Alzheimer's disease. One of the food lifestyles that have been studied extensively is the Mediterranean diet, which consists of fruits, vegetables, and lean proteins. The Mediterranean diet has also gained attention in the world of Alzheimer's disease. Some work was done at Cornell School of Medicine in New York comparing the impact of Mediterranean food versus Western food (containing red meat, saturated fat, and simple sugar) on the brain. Before and after brain images of the two groups showed that the brains of those who lived on Western diet had more buildup of beta-amyloid, which are seen in the brain of Alzheimer's patients, than those who ate Mediterranean diet. Additionally, the Western diet group had lower energy levels, thought to be a sign of slower brain activity. These contrasts suggest early development of Alzheimer's disease in the non-Mediterranean diet group.

ANTIOXIDANTS

This next study was a large Physicians Health Study that tested vitamin supplements, specifically antioxidants, for prevention of heart disease and cancer. Coincidently, they found that when used for extended period of at least ten years, and in combination with other preventive measures, antioxidants can be beneficial in lowering Alzheimer's risk. However, there are subsequent studies that do not support these previous findings.

SOCIAL ENGAGEMENT

Some studies show that being socially engaged in mid-life and later can lower the risk of dementia by up to 50%. Social engagement activities that include board games, group discussions, and social networks have shown that the more social participation an individual has, the lesser dementia risk and the less social involvement and interaction, the higher tendency for dementia.

5

Using Food to Lower Dementia Risk

I made a lot of changes to my eating habits in my journey to prevent Alzheimer's disease. Because I had a strong desire to help myself, I made changes that I never in my wildest dreams thought I could make. As someone of African descent, I loved meat so much. I enjoyed chicken, goat meat, and beef. All my three meals a day must contain some form of meat. But I finally made a conscious effort to give up meat. As at the time of writing this chapter, I have not had meat for almost two years. This was a huge accomplishment for me. I replaced my meat with fish plus other seafood and other high protein meals such as tofu and protein drinks and protein bars. It was not necessarily an easy change, but it was not difficult cither. I have not wanted to go back to eating meat since I gave it up.

The next group of foods that I gave up, or at least cut down on significantly, are sugar and carbohydrates. Sugar in this context means both refined sugar like sugar cubes, white sugar, sugary drinks, candy; and complex sugar found in flour, white rice, and potatoes. It also includes fruits with high sugar contents such as mangoes, grapes, pineapple, cherries, and watermelon. Changing these sweet-tasting foods and replacing them with different healthier foods requires discipline and adaptation, but eventually, it becomes second nature. Now I get a sick feeling to my stomach when I attempt to drink high sugary drinks like latte, chocolate, soda or when I eat white rice or pizza. Don't get me wrong, I do indulge myself with these 'not so good' foods every now and then when I can tolerate them, especially when I go out with friends. But it's not a lifestyle for me. It is also reasonable for you to yield to some cravings, especially during social gatherings, but it should be the exception and not the rule. Occasionally, you will fall off the wagon, but you need to get back up and stick to the plan.

Certain foods, which I have listed below, are healthy for the brain, and other foods, as pointed out above, are unhealthy for the brain.

"You are what you eat" is a quote from Dr. Peter Attia, a Canadian physician, and a researcher on longevity. This quote is especially true in dementia prevention because what goes inside your body has a major impact on your brain. Brain healthy foods have both direct and indirect benefits to the brain. Eating certain foods can increase anti-inflammatory and antioxidant properties that are beneficial to the brain. It may also block amyloid plaques and tau that are seen in Alzheimer's brain. The right food can also improve the cellular function (activities within a cell) of the brain that offers protection against Alzheimer's disease. Indirectly, a healthy diet will affect common risk factors for Alzheimer's—diabetes, obesity, and heart disease—and ultimately lower overall risk for Alzheimer's disease significantly.

A. The Mediterranean diet contains **vegetables, legumes, fruits, nuts, cereals, and olive oil, low intake of saturated fats and meat**. Although it lays great emphasis on plant foods, it is not considered vegan diet. This diet has been studied extensively and found to be a brain healthy diet.

B. The MIND diet, which is a hybrid of the Mediterranean diet, includes 10 brain healthy food groups as follows: **green leafy vegetables, other vegetables, nuts, berries, beans, whole grains, fish, poultry, olive oil and a glass of wine**. Unhealthy foods that will increase dementia are *high servings of red meat, butter and margarine, cheese, pastries and sweets, fried and fast foods*. As much as possible, you should avoid *diet sodas and drinks with artificial sweeteners, French fries, doughnuts, white bread and white rice, and red meat*. These food can cause inflammation and damage blood vessels that supply blood to the brain, and this will generally hurt the brain.

MIND diet study showed that 53% of participants who consistently and strictly adhered to the diet had protection against dementia. MIND diet looks like this:

2 to 5 servings of berries per week
3 to 4 servings of whole grain meals per week
5 servings of vegetables, nuts and seeds weekly
3 to 4 servings of beans per week
At least one serving of salmon, mackerel, or sardines per week
At least 2 servings of poultry weekly
2 tablespoons of extra-virgin olive oil per day

Both the Mediterranean and MIND diets have a foundation in plant-based foods, and they have been proven to offer protective effects on your brain and physical condition. Eating healthy meals—particularly plant-based foods rich in antioxidants and unsaturated fats—can lower the amount of damage caused by toxic metabolites (which are the harmful byproducts of substances found in the body) and improve blood flow to the brain. Eating meat is not completely discouraged but it needs to be cut down significantly, because animal products have saturated fat that may increase cholesterol, which is very bad for overall health, and bad for the brain. Consider choosing poultry over red meat.

You have been told to include fruit in your daily meals but not all fruits are good for you. Some have large content of natural concentrated sugar, otherwise known as high glycemic index, and you should avoid them as much as you can.

These fruits include cherries, papayas, pineapples, bananas, oranges, watermelons, grapes, melons, raisins, mangoes, nectarines, peaches.

Look for fruits with lower natural sugar content or low glycemic index. Some of the fruits include apricots, cherry plums, blueberries, strawberries, blackberries, raspberries, lemons, grapefruits, plums.

Berries with low glycemic index and green leafy vegetables such as spinach, collard greens, kale, romaine lettuce have antioxidant properties that have protective effects on the brain

Keeping portion size in mind is also as important as choosing the right fruit or vegetable.

6

Fit Mind, Fit Body:
How Physical Activity Prevents Dementia

Y ou can exercise your body and nurture your brain.

According to Alzheimer's society, physical exercise alone can lower the risk of developing dementia by almost 30%. Exercise stimulates your heart to pump oxygen and nutrients into your brain cells. Research shows that engaging in 45-60 minutes of physical exercise several days a week or an intense quick burst of exercise will offer the most benefit to your brain. One of the benefits is slowing shrinkage of hippocampus which is the memory center of the brain.

The best time to incorporate physical activities as part of your common daily or weekly routine is now. If you are someone who finds it harder to convince yourself to go and do some work out, you are not alone. Every time I tell myself that I will be going to the gym at a certain time, I will also find flimsy reasons why I should not go on that day. I must remind myself why I should work out consistently. When it becomes a matter of protecting my brain, I know this is something that is not debatable for me. Alzheimer's disease takes away memories, independence, and ability to connect to family and friends. If regular work out spares me from this experience, I will do everything in my power to stay motivated about my work out routines, and so should you. Any activity is better than none but doing more serves a higher purpose. Also, doing the types of exercise that you enjoy allows you to maintain a routine.

These exercises feed the brain tissue nutrients to regulate blood flow. In general, your brain needs:

1. Muscle strengthening exercises at least three times per week. Typical examples are squats, lunge, deadlift, crunch, bicep curl, resistance band exercises, etc.
2. 150 minutes of weekly moderate intensity exercise or 75 minutes of weekly high or vigorous intensity exercise or both. The way to tell the two exercise intensities apart is that with moderate intensity, you can talk with ease but not be able to sing and with high vigorous intensity, you cannot say much without gasping for breath.

Examples of moderate intensity exercises are:

> Riding a regular or exercise bike, cardio machines, dancing (any type that gets you moving to a fast beat such as salsa and tango), hiking, water aerobics, brisk walking, yard work.

Examples of vigorous intensity exercises are:

> Running faster than 5 miles per hour, jumping rope, hiking uphill, swimming laps, vigorous aerobic dancing, playing soccer or basketball

Even when you cannot engage in moderate or vigorous exercise, it matters to move around often, at least after sitting for a couple of hours. Sitting several hours a day tends to increase the thinning of the medial temporal lobe of the brain and this thinning can contribute to dementia. If one cannot engage in adequate physical activities as recommended due to other physical challenges, then you should be as physically active as your situation and conditions allow. You can incorporate physically fun activities in your everyday life. Some activities and hobbies you can try or include are:

> Dancing, fishing- Yes, fishing is both a hobby and physical activity. Anglers, or those who fish with hook and line, use hand and eye coordination; they strengthen the muscles in

their shoulders, hands and wrists, hiking, jogging, Pilates, yoga

I started with a personal trainer that assisted me in choosing
the best work out routines for me. I highly recommend it if
you are having a hard time getting started. If you already
have a good workout routine that you enjoy, stick to it. The
most important thing is to find something you enjoy and to
keep at it.

7

Boost your brain by enhancing your memory skills

It has been inferred based on animal studies and ongoing human studies that having brain activity can reduce the amount of brain damage on a cellular level, some of which are often associated with Alzheimer's. Brain activity can also support growth of new nerve cells as well as promote communication between nerve cells. Challenging your brain regularly and staying mentally engaged will protect your brain as you advance in age, improving your memory and thinking cells. Keeping your brain stimulated in a positive manner will reduce certain age-related forgetfulness and brain fog.

This next chapter will describe all the ways to improve our brain function and keep our memory cells intact.

There are several activities that promote mental stimulation, improve brain function, and build your cognitive reserve.

Reading should be part of your life. When I was in high school, I used to read lots of novels, especially fiction. But I gave it up when life got too busy. I have rediscovered reading in my middle age, and it brings me so much joy. I can honestly say that reading helped me to also rediscover writing. Reading can improve cognitive function and retention. It can lower anxiety by keeping the mind active and engaged while strengthening your ability to stay focused. Reading improves creativity and problem-solving skills. Reading also offers peace of mind and improves sleep quality.

Meditation is a wonderful tool that helps to reduce stress and anxiety. It is a personal experience, so that what works for one may not work for the other. Most meditation practices produce calm. You find a personal space and position that is quiet and comfortable, use some breathing techniques and take yourself on a journey of the mind. The result is peace and tranquility that can sustain you through the day or night depending on when you do it. Overall, there are 10 known meditation types or forms:

- Breathing
- Mindfulness
- Focus
- Movement or walking

- Cultivation (bring awareness, develop the mind, and connect with the senses and life experiences)
- Christian
- Buddhist or other Spiritual
- Guided
- Transcendental
- Progressive Relaxation

There are many online programs that offer step by step processes of meditating. But it takes practice and patience to master meditation skills.

Adequate sleep means at least 7-8 hours of restful sleep per night. Sleeping allows our brain cells to rest and recharge. It has been proposed, and some studies have found that sleeping restfully is the key to the brain ridding itself of toxins that build up during wake period. Sleep also has some protective effect on Parkinson's disease, stroke, and other brain disorders. Some people struggle to sleep and some of the reasons could be related to stress, long screen time, medications, or health conditions. It is important that you deal with the root causes of your sleep deprivation or poor sleep pattern and work toward improved sleep quality.

Learn and practice **a new skill** or rediscover old ones. As I mentioned earlier, I used to read a lot of novels when I was in my teens, and I loved to write short stories in my younger adult years, but life happened, and I gave them up.

Fortunately, I have rediscovered them and they have brought so much joy to my life.

Examples of skills worth looking into include:

Crossword puzzles
Gardening
Knitting & Crafting
Chess
Puzzles
Drawing
Music
Cooking (Brain healthy meals)
Reading
Writing

Group support and social activities: have social gatherings with friends and family and have positive interactions. Avoid conversations that bring divisions or keep them to a minimum. Both introverted and extroverted personalities can find social comfort levels. I used to be a social butterfly in my younger years. When I turned 40, I trained myself to become more inward facing, and I cut down significantly on non-revitalizing company kept. You could say I became more introverted. But with everything I know about preventing dementia or cognitive decline, I have had to restructure my social life again. I still do not keep many 'friends' but I can find a balance between being very strict at keeping just a few friends and socializing with a large group.

Treat Depression and Manage stress: There are several effective treatments for depression. Stay connected with your health care provider on any depression related issues and other mental health matters. Everyone manages stress differently. Know what works for you during stressful situations. Learn coping styles and other stress management skills and practice them regularly. Some activities also discussed here are useful for dealing with stressful situations

Learning **a new language** can improve retention and boost memory. It is also an activity that stimulates brain cells to communicate to the rest of the body

Lifelong learning. Staying educated on anything whenever the opportunity is presented is an attractive habit.

When you keep your brain active with exercises or other tasks, you may help build up a reserve supply of brain cells and links between them. You might even grow new brain cells. This may be one reason scientists have seen a link between Alzheimer's and lower levels of education. Experts think the extra mental activity from education may protect the brain by strengthening connections between cells.

Brain Applications (Brain apps)

They are developed to help you exercise your mind while having fun at the same time. They work by increasing blood flow in different parts of the brain and therefore allow for faster responses and memory recall. Brain Apps are available on your phones and computers. There are five that have their way into the mainstream. They are Lumosity, Peak, CogniFit, Memorado, and Elevate.

Lumosity has been around for years and has a lot of subscribers. You can exercise your memory, increase your speed of processing information, and at the same time, improve your problem-solving skills

Peak is short and intense brain workouts. There is a virtual personal trainer who encourages and challenges new exercises and keeps track of your progress. The trainer also shows you how and areas where you can improve your skills

CogniFit or cognitive fitness games improve contextual and working memory, concentration, processing speed, planning, naming objects or people, response time, etc.

Memorado is a way to create new memories, learn new skills, and improve language and vocabulary skills. Memorado is said to work by sharpening IQ using some personalized games and some mental exercises

Elevate has different learning activities that help to improve cognitive and analytical skills including but not limited to reading, writing, speaking, math, focus, and attention.

For each of these apps, you may go to the app store (Apple Store for iPhones and Macs and Play Store for Android devices) on your smartphone or iPhone, tablet or iPad, or laptop or desktop. Type the name of any of the apps above. Install the app on your device. Open the downloaded app and access the games.

8

The Time Is NOW! Why Immediate Action Matters

B eing proactive in adopting a lifestyle of risk mod-ification should intensify during mid-life (45-65). The grace period of 10 years of amyloid plaques deposit in the brain warrants adopting a preventive strategy for Alzheimer's before symptoms start to manifest. You can stop amyloid plaques from building up by starting earlier on in life; by intentional and making concerted effort about adopting preventive brain health measures.

If I knew then what I know now, I probably would have started in my thirties to adopt the changes I now have in my life. But I also realize that it may not have been realistic at that busy stage in my life when I was trying to build a career and raise my children. Whatever stage in life you are, it is alright to start now because inaction will increase your chances of developing Alzheimer's disease.

I have talked to friends whose parents have or had dementia. I have also told the story of my own mom's journey with dementia. What we all have in common is the fact that most of our parents did not take preventive measures against Alzheimer's. The reason for this varies from lack of information or knowledge about these measures and the fact that they were not a bit concerned about Alzheimer's disease during their younger years. But things are different now. We have the information at our fingertips, and it's all embedded in using what we know from science to develop ways we can lower our risks of Alzheimer's. The time is now; don't wait for symptoms to be present before you start thinking about preventing them.

But don't feel overwhelmed. A journey of a thousand miles begins with a step. In this journey, you just need to start. If you start and stop, start again. Do not try to start everything at once so you do not get overwhelmed. You can start slowly but increase the frequency, and consistency gradually. Don't get stuck in one accomplishment. Keep moving and do not give up. To keep an active life, you begin by picking any form of exercise you think you will either enjoy or tolerate. Be consistent with it and add to it when you have become comfortable. I do 45–60 minutes gym work out 4 days a week; I take walks on non-work out days if weather permits. Perhaps you can consider building up to routines like this.

Pay attention to what you consume. See if the Mediterranean diet or MIND diet works for you. If you are a meat eater, keep it to a minimum and avoid red and processed meat if possible. Cut off refined sugar from your meals.

A dear friend once visited me and my mom in my home when I was my mom's caregiver, and he said: "I have always prayed for long life when I should be praying for long life with sound mind." Remember to put those prayers for long life with a sound mind into action. Here are some specific steps that you can start to take immediately:

- Learn something new, such as a second language or a musical instrument. I will recommend learning a language or musical instrument that you will use in real life situations.
- Play board games with your kids or grandkids. Get your friends together for a weekly game of cards. Mix it up by trying new games. The extra bonus of activities like these social connections also help the brain.
- Work on crosswords, numbers, or other kinds of puzzles.
- Play online memory games or video games.
- Read, write, or sign up for local adult education classes. Participate in monthly book clubs.

- Quit smoking with resources available to you. Nicotine replacement therapy, bupropion, varenicline and behavioral interventions are available at your disposal by checking with your health care provider.
- Drink less alcohol or give it up completely.
- Eat healthy meals, especially MIND or Mediterranean diets. Add whole grains. Don't forget portion sizes. Avoid fast foods.
- Maintain a reasonably healthy weight.
- Keep blood pressure and blood cholesterol under control.
- Keep your blood sugar under control. Adhere to diabetes treatment if you are a diabetic.
- Minimize stress. Pick your battles and walk away from situations that do not add value to your wellbeing.
- Sleep Restfully for 7–8 hours.
- Stay socially active. Engaging in a social activity is a brain booster.
- Cut down on benzodiazepines and anticholinergics such as Diphenhydramine found in over the counter Tylenol PM.
- Stay physically active and exercise routinely. Focus on strength and cardiovascular training. Build high stamina and high muscle mass.

I have come across individuals who think that there is absolutely nothing anyone can do to avoid getting Alzheimer's dementia if you are destined to get it. I once joined a caregiver Alzheimer's support group on Facebook where people talked about their emotional difficulties taking care of someone with the disease. Some of the caregivers in the group are middle-aged women and direct family members of the patients. I remember someone asked the question of what could be done to prevent them from having this disease and not experience what their parent was going through, and especially not putting their own children through the same experience of being the sole caregivers. A few people who responded, told them, "There's absolutely nothing you can do." This was of course, a lot of misinformation. I had to leave the group because it made me very sad to read such negative comments. All this happened before I started writing this book. The good news is that I plan to go back to the group and find a way to educate people and bring some of the hope that I believe people desperately need.

9

Your Questions answered

1. **Does hormone replacement therapy play any role in Dementia prevention?**

The short answer is No. Hormone Replacement therapy (HRT) studies published in the Journal of Frontiers in Aging Neuroscience show that HRT might be beneficial if started about ten years before women start going through menopause. This is explained by the fact that the brain can handle positive benefits of estrogen, which may include slowing cognitive decline. Other studies do not support the beneficial use of HRT against dementia. These studies do show that HRT may increase the risk of dementia, especially if it is started and/or continued after menopause. Because studies that are currently available have conflicting results, hormone replacement therapy is not recommended for prevention of Alzheimer's.

2. Which supplements offer the most protection against Dementia?

There are numerous supplements that play various roles in protecting human organs and systems. Calcium and vitamin D for instance are essential for bone health, as in offering protection against osteoporosis. Antioxidants supplements such as beta carotene, vitamin A, vitamin C, and vitamin E may be useful for protection against damage of cells by free radicals. For those who already have dementia, vitamin E has some benefit in slowing it from progressing quickly. In dementia prevention studies, vitamin E and vitamin C supplements have some positive effects on the brain, but only when used for more than ten years. However, other studies do not show the same positive benefit but do show that high content of beta carotene may have bad health outcomes. Therefore, unless you take these supplements because they were recommended by your doctor for other conditions, there is no justifiable reason for using these supplements routinely for dementia prevention. If you have healthy eating habits, your meal consumption should have adequate content of antioxidants.

3. What roles do B vitamins and folic acid play in preventing dementia?

Vitamin B12, folic acid, and usually vitamin B6 supplements were initially thought to prevent and slow memory decline, but this is no longer the case. These supplements do not prevent dementia but as discussed in chapter 3, low levels of B vitamins, especially vitamin B12, may mimic dementia. Therefore, if someone has low levels of vitamin B12, they need to take supplements to get their levels within normal range before diagnosis of dementia can be positively made.

If you are already taking these vitamins for other reasons and to the advisement of your health care provider, then you may continue to do so. But if you want to keep things simple, you do not need to take these vitamins specifically for dementia prevention

4. **I already take Omega-3 fatty acids, and I would like to continue taking it even if it is not recommended. Does it offer any cognitive protection?**

It has been shown that having some omega 3 in the blood cells can improve brain function among those in their 40s and 50s. Omega 3 fatty acids have 2 micronutrients called docosahexaenoic acid (DHA) and eicosatetraenoic acid (EPA) which are known to enhance brain function. It is also shown that DHA and EPA are protective against APOE4 (Alzheimer's gene). You can get adequate omega-3 from cold water fish such as salmon, mackerel, and especially sardines. You can also get it from nuts, seeds and eggs. If you do not have an adequate intake of omega-3 rich foods, then you should take omega-3 supplement for cognitive protection, but you need not do both.

5. Does Ketogenic diet have any place in Dementia prevention?

There have only been a few newer studies done to see if ketogenic diet has any place in dementia prevention. Ketogenic (or keto) diets are high fat, low-carb and moderate protein meals. The goal of ketogenic diets is to get most of daily energy intake from fat and proteins and less from carbohydrates and convert them into ketones. In the studies, ketogenic diet was intended to reduce dependence on glucose as a means of energy supply to the brain and use ketones. Different studies produced different conflicting results. At this point in time, there is no convincing evidence to show that a ketogenic diet can prevent dementia

6. Do statins lower the risk of dementia?

Statins are a class of medications primarily used to lower cholesterol levels and heart conditions. Common statins include Atorvastatin (Lipitor), Simvastatin (Zocor), Rosuvastatin (Crestor), Fluvastatin (Lescol), and Lovastatin (Mevacor). Studies show that statins indirectly have the potential to reduce the risk of dementia. But this is largely true for those who are being treated with statins for high cholesterol. By reducing cholesterol levels, statins will automatically lower amyloid plaque and inflammation in the brain. Additionally, use of statins will minimize risk of stroke, and the absence of stroke will prevent the negative consequences of stroke on dementia. On the other hand, statins are not currently being recommended for dementia prevention on those in their middle-aged who do not have cardiovascular indications for statins.

7. **Should I consider genetic testing to better understand my dementia risk?**

The APOE4, the Alzheimer's gene, tells you if you are at higher risk of Alzheimer's disease based on how many copies of the gene you have. It will not predict whether someone will have the disease or not. Experts advise avoiding taking the test as it is most likely to influence you into making negative life decisions if the result is positive. I took the expert advice and steered away from taking the test myself. If you have a parent who had early onset Alzheimer's, which happens between 40-65, I think it is proper to have a conversation with your doctor on whether it is in your best interest to take the test. Before you do the test, you should have plans in place to receive genetic counseling that includes a plan on what you should do with a positive test result.

8. **How can I educate my family members about dementia prevention, especially if we share the same risk factors?**

Buy this book for your family members. This is why I wrote the book. I have tried to simplify a lot of the research and information out there for the non-health care professionals such as your loved ones.

Are there any clinical trials or studies that I could partic-ipate in to help with research? Yes.

NIA-Funded Active Alzheimer's and Related Dementias Clinical Trials and Studies | National Institute on Aging (nih.gov)

10

My Weekly Customized Brain Health Strategy

L ike I discussed in most of the book, I did not pay attention to the impact of dementia on the patient and patient's family until dementia came knocking on my family's door. I believe most people have the mindset that if something does not affect them directly, they have no business doing anything about it. That was how I felt even though I came across patients with dementia on a regular basis. I am glad that I have reexamined my own life and lifestyle, and I have made some changes that would likely benefit me in the long run and lower my risk of dementia. The following is my personalized approach that I have taken from the perspective of a health care professional, middle-aged mom, wife and daughter of a mom with Alzheimer's disease. Feel free to modify for your own life situation as necessary.

FOOD:

**Foods I used to enjoy but
found alternatives to:**

This was in line with the MIND diet. This diet was developed especially for the brain and prevention of neurodegeneration and so it would be brain-wise to try and follow it. With this, I found alternatives to the following: All types of meat including beef, chicken, bacon, turkey, goat meat. Most dairy products such as milk, cheese, eggs. I avoid these because they are animal products. Foods with high sugar content such as cake, chocolate/vanilla drinks, latte, mocha, all sodas, watermelon, banana, orange, mango, pineapple, plantains. Foods with high starch content such as potatoes, flour, yam, white bread, white rice. Foods with high fat content such as butter, margarine, vegetable oil, shortening, palm oil. I replaced them with all the alternatives given in the MIND diet. See chapter 5 for the diet staples.

Foods that I eat either daily or weekly:

Fish such as salmon, sardines, stockfish, shrimp.

Olive oil for my regular cooking and any frying.

Tofu, black eye peas, melon seeds or melon soup in moderation, boiled peanuts in moderation.

Protein bars with at least 20gm protein and less than 2gm sugar/serving.

Whole grain/whole wheat bread (1 slice).

Brown rice (in moderation), Quaker Oats.

Green peas snacks

My Vegetables are Spinach, kale, carrots, green beans.

My Fruits are blueberries, strawberries, black berries, and raspberries.

Supplements that I take

Calcium with Vitamin D.

Multivitamin with minerals.

HABITS

Things I stay away from:

Smoking. I have never smoked, and I stay away from second-hand smoke, which also includes hanging around BBQ grills and smoking meats.

Alcohol. I do not consume alcohol, but when I remember it, I would consume a small glass of red wine once a week as a protective mechanism for the brain and heart. Sometimes I forget, simply because I am not a person who keeps alcohol in the house.

Physical exercise

I contracted with a personal fitness trainer for three months, meeting with him four times a week for 45-minute training sessions.

I have a gym membership that I use 3–5 times per week, spending an average of one hour per routine visit.

I usually do 20 minutes of cardio on the treadmill, and I spend my remaining time doing weight lifts and leg work as much as I can tolerate.

I take daily walks for about 30-minute on days with good weather.

Brain (memory) exercise

I hired a piano teacher for three months for a one hour weekly piano lesson. On my own I play the piano for 1 hour two times per week. I still cannot read music.

I spend a couple of hours reading a book at least four times a week and based on the length of the book, I try to finish one book within two weeks.

I buy puzzles word search books from Amazon and spend at least an hour every day on them.

Social exercise and interaction:

I have a long happy conversation with my best friend at least once a week.

I have regular social interaction with community and work friends.

I have happy interactions with my family daily.

I hang out with people that have similar aspirations/personality as myself.

I intentionally avoid people that do not bring me peace and joy.

I create boundaries and stick to them most of the time.

I limit the time I spend on the screen to 2-3 hours a day except if it is work related.

I avoid watching bad news as on TV or social media as much as I can.

I watch a movie from start to finish once a week.

I write articles that I can publish in science journals, or I just write for the sake of writing, even if it's nonsense.

My Pastimes and hobbies:

I volunteer internationally, nationally, and locally and offer my services to those who are vulnerable.

I take a vacation at least once a year.

I make extra time for fun when I attend conferences and conventions.

My next steps:

Create or join a book club.

Learn another language.

Learn another musical instrument.

Join my church choir if they let me.

Improve my meditation skills.

CONCLUSION

People who have had the experience of caring for a family member with Alzheimer's dementia (or other dementias) understand firsthand the complexity of the disease, the difficulty of coming to terms with losing one's brain functions, and the resulting physical, emotional, and financial consequences for the patient and their family members. I write from the experience of having a mother who is living with Alzheimer's dementia. Your mother or father or uncles and aunts may have had to live with the disease, but you, if you do not have it, do not have to. You may have also lost your parents before they reached age 65 and wonder if the disease runs in your family. The fact is that everyone has some form of risk factor for dementia, whether it is through non-modifiable risks such as age, gender, family history, people of color, or modifiable risks such as poor dietary consumption, physical, emotional, and neurological inactivity/inadequacy. The good news is that you have the power to do something to lower those risks—to prevent yourself from having to live the life of someone with dementia. Choose the right physical activities that meet the goal of minimum

150 minutes of weekly moderate or 75 minutes of weekly vigorous exercise; be aware of the types of food you feed your body, because most of them have impact on what happens to your brain; and engage in ongoing mental exercise that challenge your brain and keep your brain cells active and prevent memory loss and mental decline. This is the way to live a healthy life and look forward to aging with intact brain function.

REFERENCES

1   Levine H. 6 Things You Should Be Doing to Prevent Dementia. Available from: oprahdaily.com. Published online: May 16, 2024.

2   Alzheimer's Research UK. Reducing your Risk of Dementia. Available: alzheimersresearchuk.org. Updated September 2023. Accessed: March 8, 2024

3   Siddarth P, Burggren A, Eyre H, et al. Sedentary behavior associated with reduced medial temporal lobe thickness in middle-aged older adults. *PLOS ONE*. Published: April 12, 2018. Available: https://doi.org/10.1371/journal.pone.0195549. Accessed: May 1, 2024.

4   Press D, Alexander M. Prevention of dementia. *UpToDate*. May 21, 2024

5   Larson Eric B. Risk factors for cognitive decline and dementia. *UpToDate*. May 17, 2024

6   Grodstein, F. Estrogen and cognitive function. Estrogen and cognitive function. *UpToDate*. March 31, 2023

7   World Health Organization. Dementia (who.int) Published online March 15, 2023

8   World Health Organization. WHO Guidelines: Risk Reduction of Cognitive Decline and Dementia. Available: https://iris.who.int/bitstream/handle/10665/312180/9789241550543-eng.pdf Published online 2019. Accessed: March 21, 2024

9   Yassine HN, Samien C, Livingstone KG, et al. Nutrition state of science and dementia prevention: recommendations of the

Nutrition for Dementia Prevention Working Group. *The Lancet* July 2022;3

10 Sommerlad A, Kivimäki M, Larson EB *et al*. Social participation and risk of developing dementia. *Nat Aging* 2023; **3**: 532–545. Available: https://doi.org/10.1038/s43587-023-00387-0. Accessed: March 12, 2024

11 Livingston G, Huntley J, Sommerlad D, Ames C *et al*. Dementia prevention, intervention, and care: 2020 report of the Lancet Commission. *The Lancet* 2020; 396 (10248): 413-446.

12 Hack EE, Dubin JA, Fernandes MA, et al. Multilingualism and Dementia Risk: Longitudinal Analysis of the Nun Study. *J Alzheimers Dis.* 2019;71(1):201-212. doi: 10.3233/JAD-181302. PMID: 31322560.

13 Alzheimer's Association. 2019 Alzheimer's Disease Facts and Figures Report. *Alzheimers Dement.* 2019: 15(3): 321-387

14 Center for Disease Control (CDC). Minorities and Women are at Greater Risk for Alzheimer's Disease: Alzheimer's Disease and Healthy Aging. Minorities and Women Are at Greater Risk for Alzheimer's Disease | CDC

15 Baker, L.D., Skinner, J.S., Craft, S et al. "Aerobic exercise reduces phosphorylated tau protein in cerebrospinal fluid in older adults with mild cognitive impairment. Alzheimer's & Dementia". July 2015; 11: 324. Available: https://doi.org/10.1016/j.jalz.2015.07.467. Accessed: May 10, 2024

16 Rakesh G, Szabo ST, Alexopoulos GS, et al. Strategies for dementia prevention: latest evidence and implications. *Therapeutic Advances in Chronic Disease.* 2017;8(8-9):121-136. Available: doi:10.1177/2040622317712442. Accessed: June 4, 2024

17 Center for Disease Control (CDC). "Alzheimer's Disease and Healthy Aging. Lifestyle behaviors can lower your risk of dementia". CDC. Lifestyle behaviors can lower your risk of dementia | CDC

18 Center for Disease Control (CDC). Alzheimer's Disease and Healthy Aging: Alzheimer's Disease and Related Dementias". CDC. What is Alzheimer's Disease? | CDC

19 Center for Disease Control (CDC). Alzheimer's Disease and Healthy Aging. Data and Statistics. https://www.cdc.gov/aging/dataandstatistics/index.html

20 Ngandu T, Lehtisalo J, Solomon S, et al. "A 2-year multidomain intervention of diet, exercise, cognitive training, and vascular risk monitoring versus control to prevent cognitive decline in at-risk elderly people (FINGER): a randomized controlled trial". The Lancet. 2015; 385 (9984): 2255-2263. Available: https://doi.org/10.1016/S0140-6736(15)60461-5. Accessed: March 5, 2024.

21 Biazus-Sehn LF, Schuch FB, Firth J, et al. Effects of physical exercise on cognitive function of older adults with mild cognitive impairment: A systematic review and meta-analysis. *Arch Gerontol Geriatr*. 2020 Jul-Aug; 89:104048. Epub 2020 May 12. Available: Doi: 10.1016/j.archger.2020.104048. Accessed: June 2, 2024

22 Siddarth P, Burggren a, Eyre H. Sedentary behavior associated with reduced medial temporal lobe thickness in middle-aged and older adults | *PLOS ONE*. April 12, 2018. Available: https://doi.org/10.1371/journal.ponc.0195549. Accessed: June 15, 2024.

23 Satizabal C, Himali J, Beiser A, et al. Association of Red Blood Cell Omega-3 Fatty Acids with MRI Markers and Cognitive Function in Midlife – The Framingham Heart Study. *Neurology*: October 2022. Available: https://doi.org/10.1212/WNL.0000000000201296. May 18, 2024.

24 Harris, Kristofer et al. 'The Impact of Routine Vaccinations on Alzheimer's Disease Risk in Persons 65 Years and Older: A Claims-Based Cohort Study Using Propensity Score Matching'. 1 Jan. 2023 : 703 – 718

25 Wallensten, J, Ljunggren, G, Nager, A. *et al*. Stress, depression, and risk of dementia – a cohort study in the total population between

18 and 65 years old in Region Stockholm. *Alz Res Therapy* **15**, 161 (2023). https://doi.org/10.1186/s13195-023-01308-4

26 Exercise Your Mind with these 5 Brain Training Apps. *The Seattle Medium*. https://seattlemedium.com/brain-apps-games-aging-health/ Accessed: October 5, 2024

Made in United States
Troutdale, OR
12/10/2024

25969998R00053